Robby Robin

THE BIRD WHO'S AFRAID TO FLY!

Richard Matrisciano

Illustrated by Brian Matrisciano

CrossBooks™
A Division of LifeWay
1663 Liberty Drive
Bloomington, IN 47403
www.crossbooks.com
Phone: 1-866-879-0502

First published by CrossBooks 10/19/2010

ISBN: 978-1-6150-7574-4

Printed in the United States of America

This book is printed on acid-free paper.

It was spring and Mr. and Mrs. Robin had just returned from their winter vacation.

"Spring is certainly my favorite time of year," chirped Mr. Robin happily. "It is a time of new beginnings."

He was perched on a branch high up in the big maple tree. From his high perch he could see houses at the edge of the woods.

"Yes, God shows us the whole world can be new again." said Mrs. Robin. She was on the branch next to him. "Like our new nest. It will be perfect for starting our new family!"

Mrs. Robin was busy arranging twigs and pieces of straw. She and Mr. Robin had been gathering them all morning.

Mrs. Robin would soon be laying her eggs. They would have to hurry. She would need the nest to hold her eggs.

"There, we have finished our nest," Mr. Robin said. His big red breast was puffed out with pride.

"And it is the very best nest ever," Mrs. Robin said smiling back.

"Yes it is," Mr. Robin said.

Before she knew it Mr. Robin flew off.

"Oh dear," she said as he left. "I wonder where he is going?"

A few minutes later Mr. Robin was back. And he brought Mr. and Mrs. Blackbird with him.

"Isn't this the nicest nest ever?" He asked showing it to the Blackbirds.

"Why yes it is," Mr. Blackbird said.

"Oh indeed, it is," Mrs. Blackbird agreed.

Mrs. Robin knew she had done most of the work. But she let Mr. Robin take the credit. She was proud of him and their nest.

Mrs. Robin settled in the new nest. Mr. Robin flew back and forth, getting food for Mrs. Robin. She would not be able to get food for herself.

On one of his trips back to the nest Mrs. Robin surprised him. There in the nest were three blue eggs!

Once again Mr. Robin puffed up his red breast. He brought all the other birds in the neighborhood to see Mrs. Robin, the nest, and the eggs. They all said it was a fine nest and they were beautiful eggs.

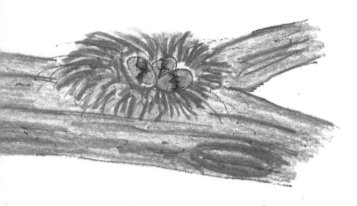

One day Mrs. Robin felt the eggs shaking. She peeked at them. They had cracks! They were ready to hatch. Soon there would be three new baby robins.

The eggs hatched. The biggest one hatched first. The middle one hatched second. And the smallest one hatched last.

Mrs. Robin was surprised. The biggest baby came out of the smallest egg. He was chubby and fuzzy. And very loud! He chirped louder than both his sisters combined.

Mrs. Robin named him Robby. She named his sisters Rona and Rena.

Soon the babies had grown. They were ready to test their wings. Rona and Rena stood on the edge of the nest and jumped. At first they began to fall. Mr. and Mrs. Robin yelled to flap their wings. When they did they began to fly!

They flew all around the tree and only stopped when their little wings got tired.

In all the excitement Mr. and Mrs. Robin forgot Robby.

"Oh dear," Mrs. Robin said. "Where is Robby?"

"I don't know," Mr. Robin said. He looked very worried.

Rona, who landed near the nest, pointed her small wing.

Everyone looked in the nest. There at the bottom of the nest was Robby. He was trying to hide under a feather.

Mr. Robin perched on the edge of the nest and moved the feather. "There you are son," he said with a smile. "It's time to test your wings. See, your sisters have already started flying."

Robby looked up at his father. "I want to stay here," he said.

"You have to fly son. That is what birds do. God has given the gift of flying to all birds. Don't be afraid."

"But I am afraid," Robby said. "If I leave the nest I'll fall."

And no matter what the family said, Robby refused to move. When his father pushed him to the edge of the nest he got dizzy and fell back into it.

"What should we do?" mother Robin asked.

"I do not know," father Robin said. "Perhaps we should push him out. He will have to fly then."

They agreed that is what they should do.

Robby was very much afraid as he was pushed to the edge of the nest. When he looked down he got dizzy again. But before he could fall back, father Robin gave him one last gentle push.

Robby was out of the nest. He was in the air. He screamed and fell like a rock. Father Robin flew after him. He flew under him and caught him just before he hit the ground.

Landing on the ground Robby hopped off his father's back.

"I'm going to stay right here," he cried. "I'm afraid of flying."

No one could convince Robby he needed to fly. Not his father. Not his mother. Not his sisters Rona and Rena. He would not fly. He stayed on the ground and walked around under the tree where he was born.

Weeks later Robby was still on the ground. He was looking for his own food. His family was busy finding food for themselves.

Just then a cat came through the trees. She lived in the house near the woods. When she saw Robby she smiled. She would have fun and scare him.

She snuck up on him as he tugged on a worm. When she was close enough she jumped out at him.

Before she could reach him she felt something hit the back of her head. It was Mr. Robin. He had been watching both Robby and the cat from the top of the tree. He was protecting his son. But the cat still chased Robby.

Mr. Robin kept pecking. Mrs. Robin flew between the cat and her son. She yelled for Robby to get away. Robby tried to run but the cat got closer.

He tried flapping his wings to run faster. Soon he was going faster than the cat. He looked back and to his surprise he saw...

He was *FLYING!*

Down below the cat turned and ran for her house, Mr. Robin chasing her all the way to the edge of the woods. Mrs. Robin flew up along side her son. Rona and Rena who had been watching flew up too.

"You're flying!" Rena said excitedly.

"Yes, I am. I am flying!" Robby shouted back.

"Aren't you afraid of being so high?" Rona asked.

Robby looked down. He was above the trees. He could see his nest below him. He had forgotten he was afraid of heights.

"I – I guess not," he answered Rona. "I am not afraid to fly!"

The entire family landed on the branch that held their nest.

"I hope you learned your lesson, young man," Robby's father said.

"Yes sir," he answered. "I was afraid to fly because I thought I couldn't. But when that nasty cat chased me I forgot I was afraid!"

"I guess we should be afraid of some things. Like that nasty cat," Robby continued. "But a bird should not be afraid of flying. God made us to fly!"

"That's right son," Robby's father said, "We should not be afraid to trust God."

"God gives gifts to all his creatures. He even gives them to boys and girls," father Robin continued.

"Are boys and girls afraid to use God's gifts too?" Robby asked.

"Yes. Sometimes even they have to be afraid before they listen to God."

"Well I will never be afraid to listen to God again!" Robby said proudly.

From that day on, Robby loved to fly. He would even forget to eat when he was flying. He even dreamed of flying when he was sleeping.

But he always said his prayers first. He even prayed for that nasty cat. And he always, *always*, remembered to thank God for the gift of flying!

The End

Lightning Source UK Ltd.
Milton Keynes UK
UKIC01n0111050914
238122UK00010B/62